# Karate

# Training

# Guide

---

## Volume 2:
### *Kata—Heian, Tekki, Bassai Dai*

**by Randall G. Hassell**

# Karate Training Guide
## Volume 2: *Kata—Heian, Tekki, Bassai Dai*

## by Randall G. Hassell

© 1991 by Randall G. Hassell
All Rights Reserved

Revised Edition
© 1997 by Randall G. Hassell
All Rights Reserved
ISBN 0-911921-23-0

Published by     Focus Publications
                 P. O. Box 15853
                 St. Louis, Missouri 63114 U.S.A.


Revised Edition
1st Printing
December 1997

**Library of Congress Cataloging-in-Publication Data**
Hassell, Randall G.
    Karate training guide / Randall G. Hassell. -- Rev. ed.
        p.    cm.
    Contents: v. 2. Kata—Heian, Tekki, Bassai Dai
    ISBN 0-911921-23-0 (pbk. : v. 2)
    1. Karate--Training.    I. Title.
    GV1114.33.T72H37    1997
    796.815'3--dc21                                97-3350

Printed in the United States of America

**Other Books by Randall G. Hassell**
**From Focus Publications**

- *Samurai Journey (with Osamu Ozawa)*

- *Zen, Pen, and Sword: The Karate Experience*

- *Conversations With the Master: Masatoshi Nakayama*

- *Shotokan Karate: Its History and Evolution (Revised and Illustrated)*

- *The Karate Spirit*

- *Karate Ideals*

- *Recognition (A Novel) with Stan Schmidt*

- *Karate Training Guide Volume 1: Foundations of Training*

# Table of Contents

# Introduction

The books in the *Karate Training Guide* series are not do-it-yourself manuals, nor are they adequate for learning karate without an instructor. Rather, these books are guides for students who already are training under a qualified instructor and who seek easy-to-follow manuals to help them in their practice.

These books also are useful for advanced students seeking review of technical points in their training.

With this in mind, these books have been written with the following objectives:

1. To provide enough technical data to get beginners started on the correct path and to serve as a reference for advanced students.

2. To provide outlines of the kata which, if students pursue them, will provide a foundation for all karate practice.

3. To provide information to instructors for the better dissemination of karate-do to the public.

# Kinesthesia

The kinesthetic sense is the movement sense. By definition it is "the sense whose end organs lie in the muscles, tendons, and joints and are stimulated by bodily tensions; the muscle sense."

The movement sense is the sense that informs us of muscular activities in the body.

The kinesthetic sense works in conjunction with the semi-circular canals in the ear, which inform us about balance, posture, and position. Thus, we know whether we are upside down or right side up. Even with our eyes closed, we are aware of movement first-hand, because sense organs that respond to movement (just as the organs of sight respond to light) are embedded in the tissue of the muscles, tendons, and joints.

As the eye receives a rich variety of impressions through light waves that stimulate light, shadow, color, hue, and intensity in the visual receptors, so we experience a wide variety of impressions through our kinesthetic sense. We are able to perceive the position of our body and the relationship of its parts. We can feel different states of tension and release in our own muscles. Through the kinesthetic sense we are aware of the speed of our movements.

Each sense has corresponding art forms that employ the materials of that sense for their media. The auditory sense has a corresponding art form—music—

whose medium is sound. Similarly, the kinesthetic sense has a corresponding art form—karate—which uses the medium of movement.

In any art form, the learning of technique is centered upon gaining mastery of the instrument and the medium. In music one is trained to control the instrument to produce subtle variations of sound. One studies the properties of sound. In music one trains the ear to learn to hear in a highly sensitive manner.

In karate, the body is the instrument and movement is the medium. It should be understood then, that karate training centers around gaining a mastery over the body and its movements. Since motion is the medium, the karate student should be concerned with the elements of motion: space, time, and energy. In karate technique, training involves learning to feel kinesthetically in a highly sensitive manner.

New students in karate usually tend to feel movement superficially. As they work kinesthetically with movement, as opposed to visually before a mirror, the muscular sensations become more definite and conscious. The more definite the perception, the greater is the depth of learning, and the more deeply the movement becomes imbedded in students' motor memories. Subtle variations in quality and shape become apparent. What was once a vague indefinite mass of movement, becomes an intricate spectrum of motion through kinesthetic training.

One of the purposes of karate training is to free the body through discipline, so that the body may move spontaneously with great skill. To come to this point requires a strong grasp on the nature of the human body and motion. An understanding of movement concepts provides a factual basis for this development. By investigating motion as a carrier of internal and external functioning, karate students extend their knowledge of themselves and their media. If karate students work with this knowledge and with heightened kinesthetic awareness, this kind of mastery can be achieved.

If the gaining of technique is an enlarging of the students' expressive means, then a technique class is an opportunity to concentrate on movement, perceive it, assimilate it, and live it.

Movement is the main material of karate. In developing and mastering its spiritual and emotional values as well as its organic functions, students build up their own bodies, so that the body becomes what it should be: the ideal instrument of the art of motion.

Students coming into karate class for the first time usually do not know they have a kinesthetic sense. Both intellectually and sensorally, they are unaware of the sense of motion.

Learning karate is a constant attempt to try to think and feel what is going on in the body. The most difficult thing to understand is that the development of karate technique is completely a matter of self-discipline. The kinesthetic sense must be trained, and this is achieved only through constant practice and study.

Kata is a valuable tool for working with the elements of movement, time, space, and energy, and it helps students gain an understanding of fundamental principles that can be used in any movement situation, so that the experience gained in one situation can illuminate another.

A karate class is an opportunity to use the body and mind creatively, and practicing karate should always involve strong physical, mental, and emotional concentration.

# The Essence of Karate Kata

Each of the major styles of Japanese karate has its roots in the old forms of Okinawa-te, the Okinawan fighting arts that were formulated largely from Okinawan and Chinese systems of combat. In its early stages of development, Okinawa-te was a system of all-out combat. There were no sport competitions; each encounter was a matter of life and death. As the systems became more stylized, the masters developed routines comprising self-defensive and symbolic movements to provide an avenue of practice for the trainee without actual combat. These routines, in turn, became highly stylized within each school and came to be known as kata (form or formal exercise).

A kata is a routine of sequential techniques performed along specified lines of movement, in which students defend themselves against multiple imaginary opponents. Each kata is a unit within itself, and each is designed to practice and demonstrate specific body movements. Some kata are slow and graceful, with long, sweeping movements, while others are fast, with short, hard movements. Some are designed to practice expansion and contraction of specific body parts, and some are designed to practice control of breathing. Regardless of the number of movements or the type of kata performed, the ultimate test of correct performance of any kata is always the same: the point at which the kata begins must coincide exactly with the point at which it finishes.

In karate kata, regardless of style, one can almost always sense beauty, coordination, and peace in the midst of turmoil.

The names of the kata are traditional and indicate the nature of the kata. *Heian*, for example, means "peaceful," and is derived from the idea that people who have mastered the five *Heian* kata are capable of defending themselves in all normal situations, and therefore have peaceful minds. *Jutte* means "ten hands," indicating that mastery of the kata gives one the strength of ten hands. *Tekki* ("Horse Riding"), *Gankaku* ("Crane on a Rock"), *Empi* ("Flying Swallow"), and *Hangetsu* ("Crescent") are named for the resemblance of their distinctive movements to commonly observed objects and actions. *Jion* is the name of a temple where the kata is reputed to have been invented, and *Bassai* means "to penetrate a fortress."

# Training in the Kata

Because the kata encompass so many of the physical techniques of karate-do, they are invaluable to student and master alike. Kata are the very essence of all karate training. They are the most effective way of practicing by oneself, and as physical conditioning exercises, they are unsurpassed. The best way to develop the muscles needed for a particular technique is to practice the technique itself. Supplementary exercises, after all, teach nothing about the techniques of self-defense. By regularly practicing the kata, students develop strength, agility, coordination, and control over their bodies. The practice of kata also is an excellent exercise in concentration. Each movement must be performed precisely. As students concentrate on each individual movement, they will be able to find for themselves many of the flaws in their technique.

As stated before, each kata is a unit within itself, and should be approached as such in training. It should not be viewed as a number of connected techniques, but rather as a single technique, in and of itself.

When approaching a kata for the first time, students should try to view the form in its entirety. Then, following the movements of a leader, perform the kata slowly several times. In this fashion, they will first gain a feeling for the general direction and timing of the form. Once the direction and timing have been learned, attention may be given to the individual movements, and they will find themselves growing stronger in the kata with each successive practice session.

From the beginning, it is very important that students understand the meaning of each movement in the kata and imagine that opponents are actually attacking as the kata movements are performed. Unless students can perform the techniques of the kata against actual attack and apply the techniques in an emergency, kata training will be useless.

Students should not practice one form exclusively and disregard the others. A well-rounded knowledge of all the kata is essential for a thorough understanding of the techniques of karate-do.

Additionally, it should be pointed out that group practice of kata is very beneficial in developing camaraderie in the dojo and precision.

### Essential Rules of Kata Training
1. View the kata in its entirety as often as possible.
2. Practice every day, even if only for a few minutes.
3. Practice each movement with a vision of the opponent in mind.
4. Breathe properly. Inhale on preparatory movements, and exhale slightly at the completion of each movement. Always concentrate breathing in the *tanden* (lower abdomen).
5. Do not rush. Try to feel each technique throughout the entire body.

# Kata Terminology

1. **Rei** - *Rei* is a ceremonial bow performed at the beginning and end of each kata. It is performed in *musubi dachi* (attention stance, toes pointing outward). Throughout the bow, the eyes remain fixed straight ahead. The bow is used to signify respect for one's opponents and symbolizes the adage of Gichin Funakoshi: "Karate begins with courtesy and ends with courtesy."

2. **Kamae** - *Kamae* is the "*yoi*" or "ready" posture from which the first movement begins. The purpose of *kamae* is to show the opponents a state of relaxed awareness. In karate *kamae*, breathe slowly in the lower stomach and concentrate on building fighting spirit.

3. **Zanshin** - *Zanshin* is the "perfect finish" of the kata and literally means "remaining mind." This means that the performer must finish at exactly the same spot where they started and that they must not relax their concentration. Spirit, mind, and concentration must remain, even after the kata is finished.

4. **Kiai** - *Kiai* is a shout from the abdomen that occurs once or twice during the kata. Its purpose is to indicate the climax of a series of movements and to help tense the body muscles through contraction of the diaphragm and the forceful expulsion of air.

5. **Embusen** - *Embusen* is the performance line of the kata. All of the *Heian* kata follow a line that is like a

large "I" or "H." All movements are performed on these lines or at sharp angles to them. Advanced kata, of course, follow much more complex lines of movement.

# Gichin Funakoshi's Three Basic Points of Kata

Following are the three basic points of kata performance as defined by Gichin Funakoshi, and they apply equally to all karate kata.

1. **Power Control *(Chikara No Kyojaku)*—**Since each kata is different and designed to demonstrate and practice different aspects of body movement, it is very important to understand where and how to apply proper strength and power in the kata. The movements are not to be done with *equal* power; they are to be done with *proper* power.

2. **Expansion and Contraction of Muscles *(Karada No Shin-Shiku)*—**This principle, again, means the *proper* expansion and contraction of body muscles, and in the *proper* order. The kata are very dynamic and complex, and performance of them must be fluid and smooth. Improper tension and relaxation will make the movements jerky and unbalanced.

3. **Speed and Rhythm Control *(Waza No Kamkyu)*—**Each kata has a different rhythm, and while some movements are performed slowly, others are performed very fast. Proper control of speed and rhythm is essential to the performance of each kata.

**Other important points include:**

4. **Deportment *(Taido)***

5. **Position and Posture** *(Shisei)*

6. **Stance** *(Tachi Kata)*

7. **Basic Techniques** *(Kihon Waza)*

8. **Line of Movement** *(Embusen)*

9. **Body Movement (Dynamics)** *(Unsoku)*

10. **Interpretation** *(Waza No Imi)*

11. **Continuity** *(Renzoku-Sei)*

# THE ORIGINS OF SHOTOKAN KARATE KATA

| NAME | MEANING OF NAME | COMMENTS |
|------|------|------|
| *Heian* (1-5) | Peaceful | Originally named *Pinan*, with 1 and 2 reversed in order. Created by Y. Itosu for use in PE classes in 1905. *Heian* is a contraction of *heian-antei* (peace and calmness). |
| *Tekki* (1) | Horse Riding | Very old Shuri-te kata, also called *naihanchi*, or Iron Horse. |
| *Tekki* (2 & 3) | | Modeled after *Tekki* 1, and created by Y. Itosu. |
| *Bassai Dai* | To Penetrate a Fortress | One of the oldest kata; also called *Patsai, Patasai* or *Passai*. Common in various forms in many styles, and can be traced back at least to ancient Oyadomari. |
| *Kanku Dai* | Sky Viewing | Ancient Shuri-te kata, common in various forms in many styles. Originally named after Kung Siang Chun (Koshokun in Japanese), a Chinese envoy to Okinawa during the Ming dynasty. Also commonly called *Kwanku, Koshokun* and *Kushanku*. |
| *Jion* | A Proper Name | Ancient Tomari-te kata, possibly brought from the Jion temple in China to Tomari. Widely practiced in Shotokan and Wado-ryu. |

| NAME | MEANING OF NAME | COMMENTS |
|------|----------------|----------|
| *Jutte* | Ten Hands | Tomari-te kata which may also be performed with a staff in the hands. Today, the empty-hand version is unique to Shotokan. |
| *Empi* | Flying Swallow | Ancient kata originally called *Wanshu*, and traceable to the 18th Century. Transmitted from Sanaeda and Matsumora to Sokon Matsumura. Practiced extensively in Tomari and developed by Kiyatake, its present form comes from Y. Itosu. |
| *Hangetsu* | Crescent Moon | Naha-te kata originally called *Seishan*. The name, *Hangetsu*, describes the crescent-like stepping pattern exhibited in the kata. |
| *Gankaku* | Crane on a Rock | Originally called *Chinto*. Taught to Sokon Matsumura by Matsumora. *Kyatake Chinto* (which features *sagi-ashi dachi*, or the sole of one foot resting against the inner knee of opposite leg) is widely practiced in many styles, while Itosu's *Chinto* (*Gankaku*), which features *gankaku dachi* (foot hooked behind the knee) is practiced only in Shotokan and Shito-ryu. |
| *Bassai Sho* | The Lesser Bassai | Created by Y. Itosu, using *Bassai Dai* as a model. |

| NAME | MEANING OF NAME | COMMENTS |
|------|-----------------|----------|
| *Kanku Sho* | The Lesser *Kanku* | Created by Y. Itosu, using *Kanku-Dai* as a model. |
| *Gojushiho Dai* | The Greater 54 Directions | Originally called *Useshi*, and re-named by Funakoshi as *Hotaku*. A Shuri-te kata taught by Y. Itosu and favored by Kenwa Mabuni and Kanken Toyama, it is today an advanced kata of both Shotokan and Shito-ryu. |
| *Gojushiho Sho* | The Lesser 54 Directions | A variation of *Gojushiho Dai*. |
| *Chinte* | Unusual (Strange) Hands | Also called *Shoin*, and believed to be an ancient Chinese kata. Practiced today in Shotokan and Shito-ryu. |
| *Sochin* | Immovable or Rooted | Probably created by Ankichi Arakaki, and originally called *Hakko*. Changed extensively by Yoshitaka Funakoshi, it is practiced today primarily in Shotokan and Shito-ryu. |
| *Nijushiho* | 24 Directions | Originally called *Niseshi*, and probably created by Ankichi Arakaki. Practiced today in Shotokan, Shito-ryu and Wado-ryu. |
| *Unsu* | Hands in the Clouds | Considered the most advanced kata in Shotokan, it contains elements from 15 different kata, and can be traced to Ankichi Arakaki. |

| NAME | MEANING OF NAME | COMMENTS |
|------|----------------|----------|
| *Ji'in* | Temple Grounds | A Tomari-te kata originally called *Shokyo*. |
| *Meikyo* | Polished Mirror | Originally called *Rohai* and divided into three separate kata, *Meikyo* may also be performed with a staff in the hands. Not taught extensively by Funakoshi, perhaps because it contains *sankaku-tobi* (triangular leap), which in old times was held to be a secret and spiritual technique. |
| *Wankan* | A Proper Name | Also called *Hito* and *Shiofu*. A very old kata of Tomari-te, traceable as far back as Matsumora. Practiced today in Shotokan and Shito-ryu. |

# The 15 Basic Kata of Shotokan Karate and their Technical Value

Listed below are the fifteen kata that Gichin Funakoshi brought to Japan in 1922 as the foundation of his karate, and the main physical value of the kata as described by Funakoshi.

| Name | Movements | Time | Main Points |
|------|-----------|------|-------------|
| Heian 1 | 21 | 40 sec. | Front stance, back stance, stepping patterns, lunge punch. |
| Heian 2 | 26 | 40 sec. | Front kick, side kick while changing directions. |
| Heian 3 | 20 | 40 sec. | Body connections in forearm blocking, backfist strike. |
| Heian 4 | 27 | 60 sec. | Balance; variation in techniques. |
| Heian 5 | 23 | 50 sec. | Balance and jumping. |
| Tekki 1 | 29 | 50 sec. | Side stance, hip vibration. |
| Tekki 2 | 24 | 50 sec. | Grasping and hooking blocks. |

| Name | Movements | Time | Main Points |
|------|-----------|------|-------------|
| *Tekki 3* | 36 | 50 sec. | Continuous middle-level blocking. |
| *Bassai Dai* | 42 | 60 sec. | Changing disadvantage into advantage by use of switching blocks and differing degrees of power. |
| *Kanku Dai* | 65 | 90 sec. | Variation in fast and slow techniques; jumping. |
| *Jion* | 47 | 60 sec. | Turning, shifting variations in stepping patterns. |
| *Jutte* | 24 | 60 sec. | Powerful hip action, use of the staff. |
| *Empi* | 37 | 60 sec. | Fast and slow movements, high and low body positions, reversal of body positions. |
| *Hangetsu* | 41 | 60 sec. | Inside tension stance; coordination of breathing with |

| Name | Movements | Time | Main Points |
|------|-----------|------|-------------|
| | | | stepping, blocking and punching; circular arm and leg movements. |
| *Gankaku* | 42 | 60 sec. | Balancing on one leg; side kick; back-fist strike. |

## All Kata Begin and End With a Bow

# Kata

# *Heian Shodan*

1. Kamae. Ready position in open leg stance.
2. Step to left downward block in front stance.
3. Right middle-level step-in punch.
4. Keeping left leg in place, pivot back to right downward block in front stance.

5. Keeping left foot in place, draw right arm and leg forcefully back.
6. Return right leg to front stance, swinging right arm in a circle over your head, striking with right bottom-fist strike at collar- bone level.

Note: Techniques 5 and 6 are one, smooth, continuous motion.

7. Left middle-level step-in punch.
8. Keeping right foot in place, turn 90 degrees to left downward block in front stance.

9. Step forward to right rising block in front stance.
10. Step forward to left rising block in front stance.
11. Without pause, step forward to right rising block in front stance. **KIAI**.
12. Keeping right foot in place, pivot around to left downward block in front stance.

13. Right middle-level step-in punch.
14. Keeping left foot in place, pivot back around to right downward block in front stance.
15. Left middle-level step-in punch.
16. Keeping right foot in place, pivot 90 degrees to left downward block in front stance.

17. Right middle-level step-in punch.
18. Left middle-level step-in punch.
19. Without pause, right middle-level step in punch. **KIAI**.
20. Keeping right foot in place, pivot around to left middle-level knife hand block in back stance.

21. Keeping left foot in place, step forward 45 degrees to right middle-level knife hand block in back stance.
22. Keeping left foot in place, pivot to right middle-level knife hand block in back stance.
23. Keeping right foot in place, step forward 45 degrees to left middle-level knife hand block in back stance.
24. Draw the left leg back to open leg stance, facing front.

## Analysis of Techniques 5 and 6

# Kata

# *Heian Nidan*

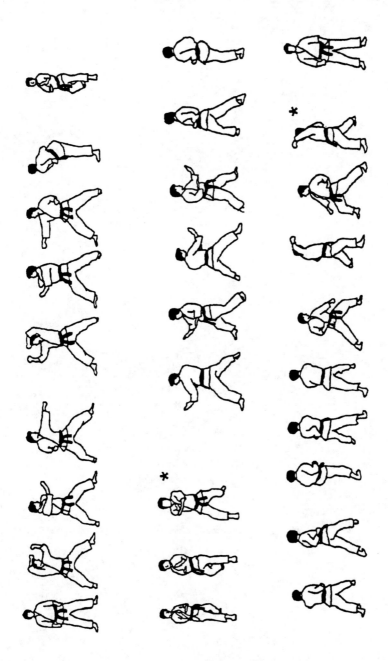

1. Slide left foot to left upper-level back forearm block in back stance. Right arm guards forehead.
2. Keeping feet in place, execute left wrist sweeping block and right bottom fist strike against opponent's elbow joint.
3. Keeping feet in place, execute left middle-level straight punch.

4. Keeping feet in place, pivot to right upper-level back forearm block. Left arm guards forehead.
5. Keeping feet in place, execute right wrist sweeping block and left bottom fist strike against opponent's elbow joint.
6. Keeping feet in place, execute right middle-level straight punch.
7. Keeping right foot in place, one-half step to right with left leg. Twist hips to right into side snap kick ready position, right hand over the left on left side. Simultaneously execute right side snap kick and right back fist strike.

8.  Step down with right foot to left middle-level knife hand block in back stance.
9.  Step forward to right middle-level knife hand block in back stance.
10. Step forward to left middle-level knife hand block in back stance.
11. Step in to simultaneous left pressing block and right middle- level spear hand thrust in front stance. **KIAI.**

12. Keeping right foot in place, pivot left middle-level knife hand block in back stance.
13. Step 45 degrees to right knife hand block in back stance.
14. Keeping left foot in place, pivot to right knife hand block to right in back stance.
15. Step 45 degrees to left knife hand block in back stance.

16. Swing left leg 45 degrees to rear in half-length front stance, executing right middle-level outward forearm block. Twist hips far to left.
17. Right front snap kick. Keep right arm in place.
18. Step down in right front stance. Left reverse punch.
19. Draw right foot back one-half step. Left middle-level outward forearm block. Twist hips far to right.

20. Left front snap kick. Keep left arm in place.
19. Step down to left front stance. Right reverse punch.
20. Right middle-level augmented forearm block in front stance.
21. Keeping right foot in place, pivot to left. Left downward block in front stance with heels in a straight line.

22. Step forward 45 degrees to right rising block in front stance.
23. Keeping left foot in place, pivot to right downward block in front stance with heels in a straight line.
24. Step forward 45 degrees to left rising block in front stance. **Kiai**.

*Tome*
Finish

Draw the left foot back and assume open leg stance.

## Analysis of Techniques 1 & 2

## Detail of Technique 16

## Detail of Technique 18

# Kata

# *Heian Sandan*

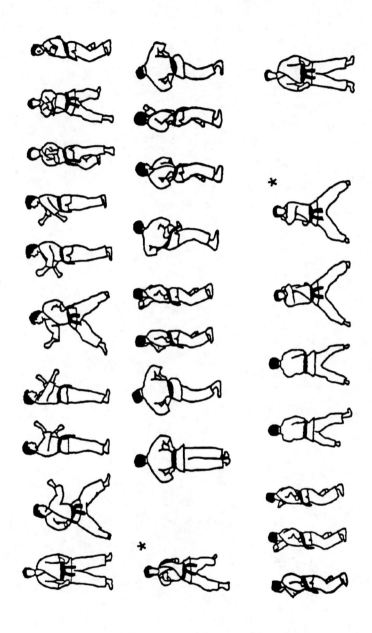

1. *Kamae.* Ready position in open leg stance.
2. Cross left arm under right, and slide left leg to left.
3. Left middle-level outward forearm block in back stance.
4. Bring right foot together with left. Simultaneous right middle- level outward forearm block and left downward block.
5. Without changing position, simultaneous left middle-level outward forearm block and right downward block.

6. Swing hips forcefully, cross right arm under left, and step to right with right foot. Right middle-level outward forearm block in back stance.
7. Bring left foot together with right. Simultaneous left middle-level outward forearm block and right downward block.
8. Without changing position, simultaneous right middle-level outward forearm block and left downward block.
9. Step 90 degrees to left middle-level augmented forearm block in back stance.

10. Step forward to simultaneous left palm pressing block and right middle-level spear hand thrust in front stance.
11. Pivot 180 degrees left on the right foot. Right open hand drops to back at belt level. Slide left foot into side stance, bringing right hand to hip in a fist. Execute middle-level bottom fist strike.
12. Right middle-level step-in punch in front stance. **Kiai**.
13. Keeping right foot in place, slowly draw left foot up while turning to face rear. Head, hands, and hips move slowly. Fists on hips.

14 Keeping hands in place, raise right knee high in front of chest, and twist hips to left.
15. Step down to right side elbow block in side stance.
16. In same position, right upper-level vertical back fist strike. Instantly return right fist to hip.
17. Keeping right foot in place, bring left knee up, as in technique 14.

18. Step down into side stance. Execute left side elbow block, left upper-level vertical back fist strike, and return fist to hip.
19. Keeping left foot in place, raise right knee as in technique 14.
20. Step down into side stance. Execute right side elbow block, right upper-level vertical back fist strike, and return fist to hip.
21. Slowly open right hand and straighten elbow, reaching toward opponent with palm down.

25. Left step-in punch in front stance.
26. Bring the right foot up even with the left, about the width of the hips.
27. Keeping the right foot in place, pivot around to the left to face the front. In side stance, keep eyes to front. Simultaneous right punch over left shoulder and left elbow strike to rear.
29. Slide strongly to right in side stance. Simultaneous left punch over right shoulder and right elbow strike to the rear. **Kiai.**
30. *Tome.* Finish. Draw right foot back toward left in open leg stance.

## Analysis of Techniques 10 & 11

# Kata

# *Heian Yondan*

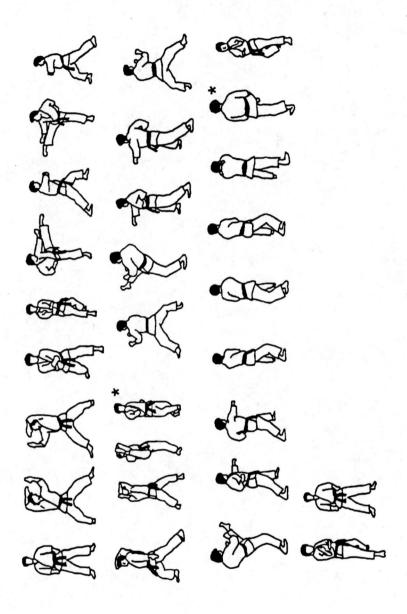

1. *Kamae*. Ready position in open leg stance.
2. Step to left in back stance, slowly swinging arms in an arc to left upper-level back-forearm block. Right hand guards front of head. Hands open.
3. Slowly swing arms in an arc to right upper-level back-forearm block. Left hand guards front of head. Hands open.
4. Keeping right foot in place, step forward to left front stance and downward X-block.

5. Step forward to right middle-level augmented forearm block in back stance.
6. Smoothly bring left foot to right knee, fists on right side (left over right), and look to left. Simultaneous upper-level back fist strike and side snap kick. Leg snaps back; arm stays out.
7. Middle-level elbow strike to palm in front stance.
8. Draw left foot back one-half step. Right foot against left knee, fists on side (right over left).Simultaneous upper-level back fist strike and side snap kick. Leg snaps back; arm stays extended.

9.  Step down to left middle-level elbow strike against right palm in front stance.
10. Look to left and execute left downward block with hand open. Right hand protects side of head.
11. Twist hips strongly to left front stance. Right knife hand strike to neck level. Left hand guards forehead.
12. Keeping hands and left foot in place, right front snap kick.

13. Land forward in front stance. Left open hand pressing block. Right hand ready to strike. Without pause, continue to slide left foot up behind right to cross-legged stance. Right middle-level back fist strike. **Kiai.**
14. Pivot on right foot to face 30 degrees to left rear, crossing both wrists in front of face. Slide into left back stance, slowly executing wedge block.
15. Keeping hands in place, right front snap kick.

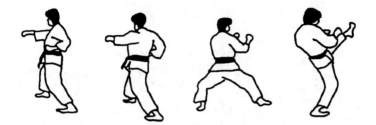

16. Land in right front stance. Right middle-level straight punch.
17. Without pause, left middle-level reverse punch.
18. Keeping left foot in place, pivot to right, bringing right foot in an arc left foot, and face 30 degrees to right rear, crossing wrists in front of face. Slide into right back stance, slowly executing wedge block.
19. Keeping hands in place, left front snap kick.

20. Land in front stance, left middle-level straight punch.
21. Right middle-level reverse punch.
22. Keeping right foot in place, swing arms to right and left foot in wide arc to left rear. Left middle-level augmented forearm block in back stance.
23. Step forward to right middle-level augmented forearm block in back stance.

24. Step forward to left middle-level augmented forearm block in back stance.
25. Keeping feet in straight line, shift body weight forward and raise open hands to face level to grasp opponent's head.
26. Bring arms down into fists beside the knee, and execute right knee strike. **Kiai.**
27. Pivot to front and land in back stance. Left middle-level knife hand block.

35. Step forward to right middle-level knife hand block in back stance.
36. *Tome.* Finish. Draw right foot back even with left to open leg stance.

## Analysis of Technique 8

## Detail of Technique 13

# Kata

# *Heian Godan*

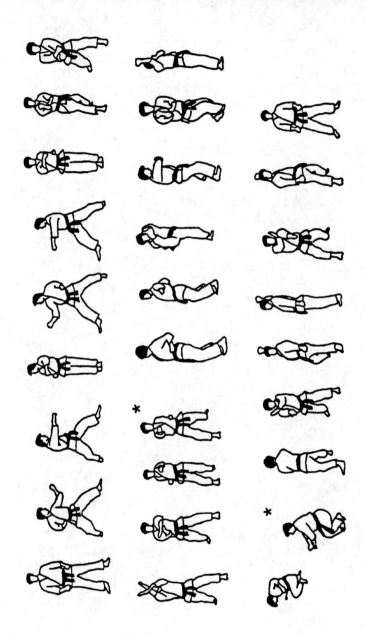

1.  *Kamae*. Ready position in open leg stance.
2.  Move left leg to left, left middle-level outward block in back stance.
3.  Without pause, right middle-level reverse punch in back stance.
4.  Slowly draw right foot toward left, swinging head, arms, and feet in unison. Left middle-level guard position.

5.  Step to right, right middle-level outward block in back stance.
6.  Without pause, left middle-level reverse punch in back stance.
7.  Draw left foot slowly toward right. Head, hands, and feet move in unison. Eyes to front, left hand on side, and right arm in middle- level guard position.
8.  Swing arms to left, and slide right foot forward. Right middle-level augmented block in back stance.

9. Step forward to downward X-block in left front stance.
10. Without changing stance, upper-level X-block with open hands.
11. Without changing stance, twist hands to wrist-to-wrist position, as if grasping opponent's hand. Without changing position, two-hand pressing block, left palm over right fist at right hip.
12. While moving forward, short middle-level straight punch.

13. Without pause, right step-in punch in front stance. **Kiai**.
14. Keeping left foot in place, pivot 180 degrees to rear, swinging right arm and right leg in a high, wide arc. Step down forcefully in side stance, right downward block.
15. Slowly execute left middle-level back hand block in side stance. Head turns in unison with hand.
16. Right crescent kick against left palm.

17. Land in side stance, facing opposite direction. Right middle-level elbow strike against left palm.
18. Facing front, slide left foot up behind right in cross-legged stance. Right middle-level augmented forearm block.
19. Turning to rear, slide left foot to L-stance. Upward augmented punch.
20. Jump to rear, turning 180 degrees in the air, tucking knees under body and pulling fists to sides. Distance covered is the length of one front stance. **KIAI** starts at top of jump.

21. Land in right cross-legged stance, knees bent as far as possible and back straight. **KIAI** ends.
22. Step to rear in right straight-line front stance. Right middle-level augmented forearm block.
23. Shift weight into left straight-line front stance. Simultaneous left sweeping block and right lower-level knife hand strike.

24. Keeping feet in position, shift weight back to back stance. Simultaneous right upper-level outward block and left downward block.
25. Keeping arms in place, slowly draw left foot up to right foot.
26. Without pause, pivot left, open arms wide, and slide right foot forward. In right straight-line front stance, simultaneous right sweeping block and left lower-level knife hand strike.
27. Keeping feet in place, shift weight back to back stance. Simultaneous left upper-level outward block and right downward block.

28. Tome. Finish. Draw right foot back even with left to open leg stance.

## Analysis of Techniques 10–12

## Analysis of Technique 14

## Analysis of Techniques 20 & 21

## Analysis of Techniques 23 & 24

## Analysis of Technique 24

## Detail of Techniques 25–27

# Kata

# *Tekki Shodan*

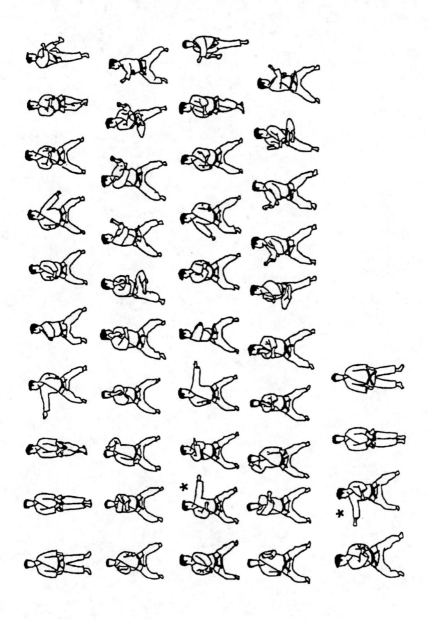

1. Kamae. Ready position in open leg stance.
2. Draw right foot next to left, left palm on top of right hand. Lower hips.
3. Simultaneously turn head to right and step in front of left foot with right foot.
4. Swing right leg high in front of body and land in side stance. Right middle-level hooking block.

5. Left middle-level elbow strike against right palm.
6. Simultaneously drop fists to right side, left on top of right, and turn head to left.
7. Left downward block to side.
8. Right hook punch.

9. Keeping arms and head in place, step to left, right foot in front of left foot.
10. Keeping head in place, raise left knee high in an arc in front of body and stretch right arm in preparation for blocking.
11. Land in side stance with right stamping kick. Simultaneously head turns to front with right middle-level outward block.
12. Smoothly cross arms in preparation for blocking, right arm inside left.

13. Simultaneous left upper-level wrist sweeping block and right downward block.
14. Left upper-level close punch. Right fist supports left elbow.
15. Keeping arms in position, strongly look to left.
16. Keeping arms and head in place, left inside snapping kick.

17. Simultaneously land in side stance and execute left middle-level reverse forearm block. Right fist under left elbow.
18. Keeping hands in place, strongly look to right.
19. Keeping arms in place, right inside snapping kick.
20. Simultaneously land in side stance and execute left inward forearm block on right side of body. Right fist under left elbow.

21. Simultaneously drop fists to right side, left fist on top of right fist, and strongly look to left.
22. Simultaneous left middle-level straight punch and right middle- level hook punch. **Kiai**.
23. Smoothly draw the left hand, palm open and down, under the right arm.
24. Slowly execute left middle-level hooking block.

25. Right middle-level elbow strike against left palm.
26. Simultaneously drop fists to left side, right fist on top of left fist, and strongly look to the right.
27. Right downward block to side.
28. Left middle-level hook punch.

29. Keeping head and hands in place, step to right, crossing left foot in front of right.
30. Keeping head in place, raise right knee high in an arc in front of body and stretch left arm in preparation for blocking
31. Land in side stance with left stamping kick. Simultaneously head turns to front with left middle-level outward block.
32. Smoothly cross arms in preparation for blocking, left arm inside right.

33. Simultaneous right upper-level wrist sweeping block and left downward block.
34. Right upper-level close punch. Left fist supports left elbow.
35. Keeping arms in position, strongly look to right.
36. Keeping arms and head in place, right inside snapping kick.

37. Simultaneously land in side stance and execute right middle-level reverse forearm block. Left fist under right elbow.
38. Keeping hands in place, strongly look to left.
39. Keeping arms in place, left inside snapping kick.
40. Simultaneously land in side stance and execute right inward forearm block on left side of body. Left fist under right elbow.

41. Simultaneously drop fists to left side, right fist on top of left fist, and strongly look to right.
42. Simultaneous right middle-level straight punch and left middle- level hook punch. **Kiai**.
43. Moving head, arms, and legs in unison, slowly draw right foot next to left foot, left palm crossed on top of right hand.
44. *Tome*. Finish. Move right leg to open leg stance.

### Analysis of Techniques 16 & 17

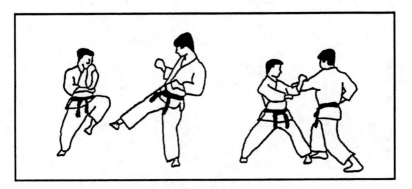

### Analysis of Technique 22

### Analysis of Techniques 31–34

# Kata

# *Tekki Nidan*

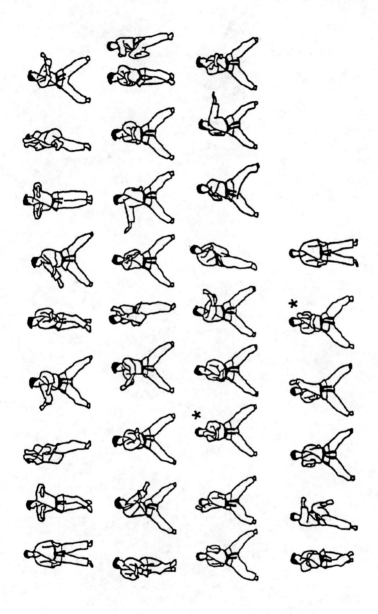

1. *Kamae.* Ready position in open leg stance.
2. Simultaneously, slowly look to right, cross left foot in front of right, and raise elbows horizontally, fists in front of nipples.
3. Raise the right foot in high arc in front of body and both arms in front of face, palms toward you.
4. Step down forcefully into side stance. Right middle-level forearm block, palm toward opponent. Left arm guards the chest.

5. Step to right, left foot in front of right. Right downward block, palm facing front. Left palm on right elbow, fingers on top, thumb below.
6. Step into side stance. Right lower-level outward forearm block, palm up. Left palm as in Technique 5.
7. Simultaneously, slowly look to left, draw left foot to right, and raise elbows horizontally, fists in front of nipples.
8. Raise the left foot in high arc in front of body and both arms in front of face, palms toward you.

9. Step down forcefully into side stance. Left middle-level forearm block, palm toward opponent. Right arm guards the chest.
10. Step to left, right foot in front of left. Left downward block, palm facing front. Right palm on left elbow, fingers on top, thumb below.
11. Step into side stance. Left lower-level outward forearm block, palm up. Right palm as in Technique 10.
12. Simultaneously look to right and drop hands to left side, right fist against open left palm, and strongly look to right.

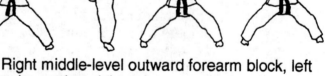

13. Right middle-level outward forearm block, left palm against right wrist.
14. Left palm covers right fist and pulls to right side. Lift right knee high in front of body.
15. Step down forcefully to side stance and execute right elbow strike to front, left palm supporting right fist.
16. Slowly execute right grasping block to right side.

17. Left middle-level hook punch.
18. Keeping head and arms in place, step to right, left foot crossing in front of right.
19. Raise right knee high and stretch left arm in preparation for blocking.
20. Land in side stance. Left middle-level outward block.
21. Simultaneous right upper-level wrist sweeping block and left downward block.

22. Upper-level close punch. Left fist under right elbow. **KIAI**.
23. Simultaneously drop hands to right side, left fist against open right palm, and strongly look to left.
24. Left middle-level outward forearm block, right palm against left wrist.
25. Right palm covers left fist and pulls to left side. Lift left knee high in front of body.

26. Step down forcefully to side stance and execute left elbow strike to front, right palm supporting left fist.
27. Slowly execute left grasping block to left side.
28. Right middle-level hook punch.
29. Keeping head and arms in place, step to left, right foot crossing in front of left.

30. Raise left knee high and stretch right arm in preparation for blocking.
31. Land in side stance. Right middle-level outward block.
32. Simultaneous left upper-level wrist sweeping block and right downward block.
33. Left upper-level close punch. Right fist under left elbow. **KIAI**.

*Tome.* Finish. Draw right foot toward left in open leg stance.

### Analysis of Technique 4

### Analysis of Technique 5

### Analysis of Technique 6

## Analysis of Techniques 14 & 15

# Kata

# *Tekki Sandan*

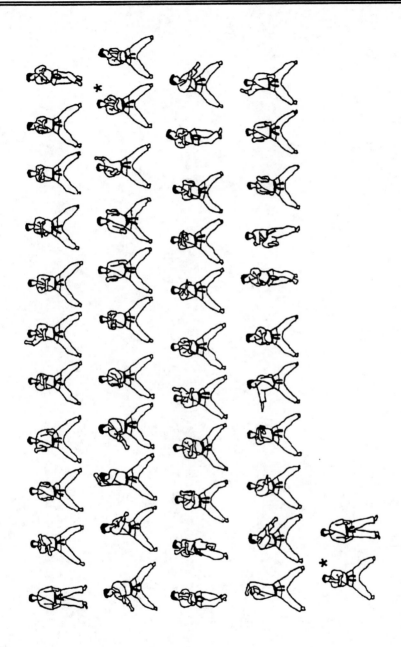

1. Kamae. Ready position in open leg stance.
2. Step to right and cross left arm under right in preparation for blocking.
3. Left middle-level outward block in side stance.
4. Crossing left arm inside right, execute right middle-level outward block and left downward block.

5. Right forearm middle block. Left arm guards chest.
6. Right upper-level wrist sweeping block. Left arm guards chest.
7. Right upper-level close punch. Left fist under right elbow.
8. Hands drop to right side, left palm covering right fist.

9.  Right middle-level straight punch. Left palm on right elbow.
10. Without pause, simultaneously turn the right fist palm up and look to right.  Left palm on right elbow.
11. Keeping hands in position, step to right, crossing left leg in front of right.
12. Right lower-level outward forearm block. Left palm on elbow, fingers above, thumb below.

13. Keeping left hand in place, draw right arm back to left.
14. Keeping left hand in place, swing right arm high overhead in an arc.
15. Keeping left hand in place, complete the swinging of the arm with the right palm down.
16. Bring both hands to right side, left palm covering right fist.

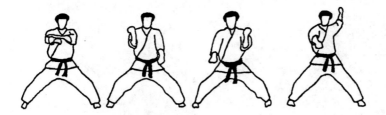

17. Without pause, right middle-level straight punch, left palm on right elbow.
18. Crossing left arm inside right, simultaneous right middle-level outward forearm block and left downward block.
19. Crossing right arm inside left, simultaneous left middle-level outward forearm block and right downward block.
20. Keeping right arm in place, left upper-level wrist sweeping block.

21. Left upper-level close punch. Right fist under left elbow. **Kiai**.
22. Forcefully look to left.
23. Keeping arms in position, step to left, crossing right foot in front of left.
24. Keeping arms in position, raise left knee in high arc in front of chest.

25. Step down forcefully into side stance and turn head to front.
26. Left forearm middle block. Right arm guards chest.
27. Left upper-level wrist sweeping block. Right arm guards chest.
28. Left upper-level close punch. Right fist under right elbow.

29. Hands drop to left side, right palm covering left fist.
30. Left middle-level straight punch. Right palm on left elbow.
31. Without pause, simultaneously turn the left fist palm up and look to left. Right palm on left elbow.
32. Keeping hands in position, step to left, crossing right leg in front of left.

33. Left lower-level outward forearm block. Right palm on elbow, fingers above, thumb below.
34. Keeping right hand in place, swing left arm high overhead in an arc.
35. Keeping right hand in place, complete the swinging of the arm with the left palm down.
36. Bring both hands to left side, right palm covering left fist.

37. Left straight punch, right palm on left elbow.
38. Right grasping block, palm down.
39. Left hook punch.
40. Keeping arms in place, step to right, crossing left leg in front of right.

41. Raise right knee in high arc in front of chest, and stretch left arm in preparation for blocking.
42. Left middle-level outward forearm block in side stance.
43. Crossing left arm inside right, simultaneous right middle-level outward forearm block and left downward block.
44. Keeping left arm in place, right upper-level wrist sweeping block.

45. Right upper-level close punch. Left fist under right elbow. **Kiai**.

*Tome*. Finish. Draw right foot back toward left to open leg stance.

## Analysis of Techniques 6 & 7

## Analysis of Techniques 8 & 9

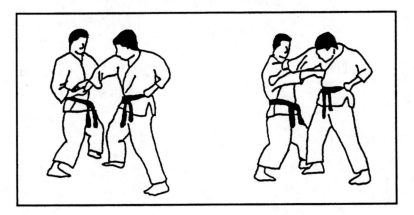

# Kata

# *Bassai Dai*

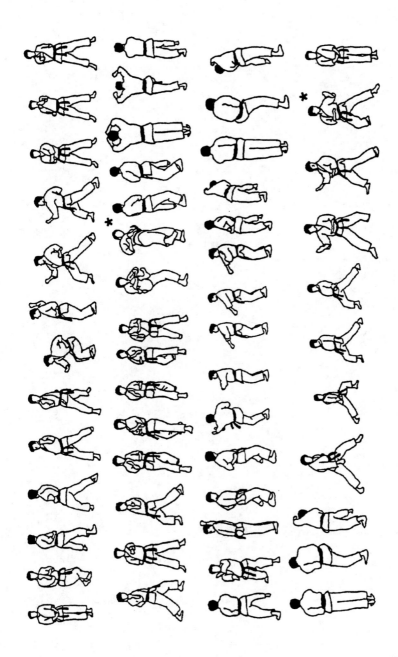

1. *Yoi.* Heels and toes together, left hand wrapped lightly around right fist.
2. Draw hands back near the side, and slide one step forward with right foot.
3. Augmented right outward forearm block in cross-legged stance. Left palm against right wrist, middle finger touching wrist bone.
4. Bring left arm under right, and turn to rear, moving left leg.

5. Left middle-level outward forearm block in front stance.
6. Keeping feet in position, cross right arm under left.
7. Right middle-level outward forearm block. Twist hips far to left.
8. Move right leg to turn to front.

9. Left middle-level inward block in front stance. Twist hips far to right.
10. Keeping feet in place, right middle-level outward block. Strongly rotate hips to left.
11. Keeping left foot in place, draw right foot back, turn to right, and execute lower-level right scooping block, palm upward.
12. Smoothly continue the motion and swing the right arm high, fist near the ear.

13. Step in with right foot, and execute right middle-level inward forearm block.
14. Keeping feet in place, execute left middle-level outward forearm block. Twist hips far to right.
15. Draw left leg back to wide natural stance, facing front, left fist on top of right on right side.
16. Slowly execute left middle-level vertical knife hand block.

17. Right middle-level straight punch.
18. Draw right fist back to left shoulder.
19. Keeping feet in place, twist strongly to left, and execute right middle-level outward block in front stance.
20. Snap hips sharply back to wide natural stance, executing left middle-level straight punch.

21. Draw left fist back to right shoulder.
22. Keeping feet in place, twist strongly to right and execute left middle-level outward block in front stance.
23. Keeping left foot in place, step forward to right middle-level knife hand block in back stance.
24. Stepping forward, left middle-level knife hand block.

25. Stepping forward, right middle-level knife hand block in back stance.
26. **Without pause**, step back to left middle-level knife hand block in back stance.
27. Keeping feet in place, drive weight forward into straight line front stance, right arm making a clockwise circle in front of the body.
28. Grasping block with both hands, palms downward. Twist hips far to left.

29. Keeping arms in place, raise right knee in between arms.
30. Strongly pull both hands to side, palms against body. Simultaneous right lower-level (knee-level) side thrust kick. **KIAI**.
31. Step down with right leg, turn to rear, and execute left middle- level knife hand block.
32. Stepping in, right middle-level knife hand block in back stance.

33. Keeping left foot in place, draw right leg back even with left (heels and toes touching), and execute upper-level block with both arms, index knuckles touching.
34. Slide right foot forward one step, arms moving apart in wide arc.
35. Middle-level bottom-fist scissors strike in front stance.
36. **Rear view**.

37. Sliding both feet forward, right middle-level straight punch.
38. Moving left leg, turn to front. Simultaneous right lower-level knife hand strike and left upper-level sweeping block. Edge of left hand touches right shoulder.
39. Slowly draw right foot back to left. Simultaneous right upper-level outward block and left downward block. Feet together.
40. Raise right knee high in front and right arm over head.

41. Right downward block to side in side stance.
42. Cross arms in front of chest, left under right, palms down, and turn head to left (rear).
43. Slowly execute left middle-level hooking block with back of hand.
44. Pivot to rear on left foot. Kick left palm with right crescent kick.

45. Land in side stance. Right middle-level forward elbow strike.
46. **Side view**.
47. Keeping feet in place, right downward block, left fist against right elbow, palm toward body.
48. Keeping feet in place, left downward block, right fist against left elbow, palm toward body.

49. **Without pause**, keeping feet in place, right downward block, left fist against right elbow, palm toward body.
50. Turn sharply to right (rear), hands in ready position on left side, right fist on top of left.
51. **Without pause**, wide U-punch in right straight line front stance.
52. **Side view**.

53. Slowly draw right foot back even with left foot, hands in ready position on right side, left fist on top of right.
54. Raise left knee high in front of body.
55. Land in left straight line front stance, wide U-punch.
56. Slowly draw left foot back even with right foot, hands in ready position on left side, right fist on top left.

57. Raise right knee high in front of body.
58. Land in right straight line front stance, wide U-punch.
59. Pivot on right leg, bringing left leg in line with right. Swing right arm high to rear.
60. Right lower-level scooping block in straight line front stance.

61. Complete scooping block by snapping arm over, palm facing upward.
62. Keep feet in place, and swing left arm high to the rear.
63. Snap hips sharply to right. Left lower-level scooping block.
64. Complete scooping block by snapping arm over, palm facing upward.

65. Bring left leg under the center of gravity of the body, and extend arms in preparation for knife hand block.
66. Step forward 45 degrees. Right knife hand block in right back stance.
67. Slowly and strongly swing right leg to 45 degree angle to right rear, keeping upper body in place. Look over the left shoulder.
68. Bring right leg under the center of gravity of the body, and extend arms in preparation for knife hand block.

69. Step 45 degrees forward with left leg. Left middle-level knife hand block in left back stance. **KIAI**.
70. *Yame*. Slowly draw the left leg back to the right, moving legs, arms, and head in unison. Assume ready position as at the beginning of the kata.

## Analysis of Techniques 26–30

## Analysis of Techniques 33–35

# DAMASHI PUBLICATIONS
### www.damashi.com • 800/563-6287

## Samurai Journey
*by Randall G. Hassell & Osamu Ozawa*
"A fascinating, honest look at a true karate master."
—*Karate-do Times*

The biography of Osamu Ozawa, the most senior Shotokan instructor in the Western world. Follow Ozawa's remarkable story, from his *samurai* upbringing, to crashing as a *kamikaze* pilot, to his run as the most successful TV director in Japan; from his rise to riches and decline into poverty, to his final triumph as a karate master. Features Ozawa's remembrances of the many influential people he's encountered including the world's greatest karate masters like Gichin Funakoshi and Kenwa Mabuni and Hollywood stars like Frank Sinatra and Rita Moreno, plus much more!
Paperback, Illustrated, ISBN 0911921249

## Conversations With the Master: Masatoshi Nakayama
*by Randall G. Hassell*
"A window of insight into the very essence and spirit of karate-do."
—*Rick Brewer, Shotokan Karate Magazine*
"Anyone who reads this book...will find cause for examining and re-examining the deeper meanings of karate-do."
—*from the Foreword by Teruyuki Okazaki, 9th dan JKA/WF*

The author was the only Western journalist to whom the late headmaster of the Japan Karate Association granted extensive, in-depth interviews for the specific purpose of writing a book. Nakayama describes his early training under the founder of modern karate, Gichin Funakoshi, and talks extensively about modern karate—where it was, where it is, and where it is going. Must reading for all serious martial artists!
Paperback, Illustrated, ISBN 0911921001

# DAMASHI PUBLICATIONS
### www.damashi.com • 800/563-6287

## Meeting Myself: Beyond Spirit of the Empty Hand
*by Stan Schmidt*
"Incredibly inspiring...A definitive representation of the true spirit of traditional karate."
—*Rick Brewer, Inside Karate*
"A story of struggle, tragedy, and triumph...Inspiring!"
—*Karate-do Times*

The autobiography of the world's highest-ranking, non-Japanese, JKA master. Re-live with Stan Schmidt almost 40 years of karate training—much of it in Japan! Share the insights he has gained from his experiences in the famous JKA Instructors' Class in Tokyo, competing against Japan's elite competitors, teaching in his native South Africa, and more! Also, read about his experiences performing in several famous martial arts movies and see remarkable photos from Schmidt's personal collection.
Paperback, Illustrated, ISBN 0911921257


## Advanced Karate-do:
## Concepts, Techniques, and Training Methods
*by Elmar T. Schmeisser, Ph.D.*
"Refreshing...Compelling...Unique..."
—*John Cheetham, Shotokan Karate Magazine.*
"...Breaks new ground...I highly recommend this book."
—*Howard High, Founder, Cyber Dojo.*

A technical book that clearly and concisely analyzes, in detail, the advanced concepts of Shotokan-style karate. Includes a large section devoted to in-breath forms of *kata*. The author, a Doctor of Medical Physiology, combines his scientific background and three decades of karate experience for the benefit of instructors and students alike.
Paperback, Illustrated, ISBN 0911921168

# DAMASHI PUBLICATIONS
### www.damashi.com • 800/563-6287

---

## Spirit of the Empty Hand
*by Stan Schmidt*

> "Stan Schmidt is the best example of what dedication to karate can do for a man...A martial gentleman."
> —*C.W.Nicol, Author, Moving Zen.*

The fascinating true story of the author's journey from the first day of karate training to achieving 3rd degree black belt in Japan. Written by the world's highest-ranking, non-Japanese, JKA master instructor.
Paperback, Illustrated, ISBN 0911921028

## The Karate Spirit
*by Randall G. Hassell*

> "Randall G. Hassell is, hands down, the world's finest, most authoritative karate-do writer."
> —*The Fighter Magazine*

A revised, selected collection of the author's popular column that originally appeared in *Black Belt* magazine for more than three years.
Paperback, ISBN 0911921192

## Zen, Pen, and Sword: The Karate Experience
*by Randall G. Hassell*

In the spirit of his bestseller, *The Karate Experience, A Way of Life,* Hassell brings to life the essence of traditional martial arts: "For me," he says, "Zen symbolizes the spiritual dimension of the martial arts, pen the intellectual dimension, and sword the physical dimension."
Paperback, ISBN 0911921133

## Karate Ideals
*by Randall G. Hassell*

A serious, thought-provoking book that examines the philosophical, historical, and societal influences on the martial arts of the samurai, and how these influences are reflected in modern-day karate training.
Paperback, ISBN 0911921184

# DAMASHI PUBLICATIONS
### www.damashi.com • 800/563-6287

---

## Karate Training Guide Volume 1: Foundations of Training
### *by Randall G. Hassell*

An illustrated guide to the basic techniques and philosophy of karate training. Clear line drawings and move-by-move instructions make this an invaluable sourcebook for beginners and advanced karate-ka alike. Includes *kata* Heian Shodan and Nidan.
Paperback, Illustrated, ISBN 0911921222

## Karate Training Guide Volume 2: Kata—Heian, Tekki, Bassai Dai
### *by Randall G. Hassell*

Complete, simple, move-by-move instructions of beginner through Brown Belt-level Shotokan-style *kata*: Heian Shodan through Godan, Tekki Shodan through Sandan, and Bassai Dai, plus detailed analysis of selected moves
Paperback, Illustrated, ISBN 0911921230

## Modern Karate:
## Scientific Approach to Conditioning and Training
### *by Milorad Stricevic; Dusan Dacic; Toyotaro Miyazaki; George Anderson*
"Authoritative...Excellent..."
*—Hidy Ochiai, 8th Dan, Washin-ryu*

Learn how to achieve peak conditioning and unbeatable competition skills—regardless of style! Over 750 photos, charts, graphs, and illustrations.
Hardcover, Illustrated, ISBN 0962201200

## Recognition (A Novel)
### *by Stan Schmidt with Randall G. Hassell*

Promising young athlete, Jonathan Walker, is felled by serious injury and thrust into a strange environment fraught with conflict and loneliness. Jonathan unexpectedly falls under the guidance of a mysterious karate master from another land.
Paperback, ISBN 0911921176

## LOOK FOR THESE FINE VIDEOTAPES AT YOUR RETAILER OR ORDER DIRECTLY FROM:

# DAMASHI PRODUCTIONS
### www.damashi.com • 800/563-6287

---

## HISTORICAL/DOCUMENTARY VIDEOTAPES

**Soul of Karate**
*Featuring Stan Schmidt, 7ᵗʰ Degree Black Belt of th*
*Japan Karate Association*

"This tape shows what the true karate spirit is about. Every
instructor must see it."
—*Masatoshi Nakayama, late Headmaster, Japan Karate Association.*

Live the essence of traditional karate training the rugged South
African way. Contains some of the most exciting karate footage ever
shot! The intriguing story never lets up in this completely restored
masterpiece documentary!
VHS, 60 MIN.
ISBN 0911921273 (NTSC); 0911921451 (PAL)


**The Winning Blow**
*Showcasing Tanaka, Yahara, Osaka, Oishi, Kagawa*
*and many other masters!*
Narrated by Stan Schmidt.

See the world's most famous karate-ka like you've never seen
them before! This fast-paced, half-hour TV program features over two
dozen Japanese karate masters in footage from the *All-Japan* and *World
Championships,* the JKA HQ in Tokyo, and much more!
VHS, 26 MIN.
ISBN 0911921281 (NTSC); 091192146X (PAL)

**DAMASHI PRODUCTIONS**
www.damashi.com • 800/563-6287

## INSTRUCTIONAL VIDEOTAPES

**Stan Schmidt Instructs SHOTOKAN KARATE**
*Volume 1: Beginner Level*

The world's highest-ranking Western instructor provides easy-to-follow demonstrations of basic techniques, *kata* Heian Shodan and Nidan, 5-step sparring, limbering, strengthening, throws, ground immobilizations, and self-defense.
VHS, 60 MIN.
ISBN 091192129X (NTSC); 0911921478 (PAL)

**Stan Schmidt Instructs SHOTOKAN KARATE**
*Volume 2: Intermediate*
*Featuring World Champion Pavlo Protopappa.*

Schmidt teaches, demonstrates, and provides practical applications of *kata* Heian Sandan, Yondan, and Godan. Includes 1-step sparring, *makiwara* training, and more.
VHS, 60 MIN.
ISBN 0911921303 (NTSC); 0911921486 (PAL)

**Stan Schmidt Instructs SHOTOKAN KARATE**
*Volume 3: Advanced for Students & Instructors*
*Featuring More Than a Dozen South African National, International, and World Champions*

The "Teacher of Teachers" returns to video with in-depth training for students and instructors alike. Includes 1-step and semi-free sparring, *kata* Tekki Shodan and Empi, advanced strength and conditioning drills, self-defense, breaking techniques, *gasshuku* (outdoor) training, and more!
VHS, 72 MIN.
ISBN 0911921311 (NTSC); 0911921494 (PAL)